Soldier Boy and the Rural Fundamentalists

Soldier Boy and the Rural Fundamentalists was completed as part of the author's role as the inaugural writer-in-residence at the Historic Hydro Hotel in her hometown of Leeton in New South Wales. Developed by Sarah herself, the program has involved living at the iconic Art Deco hotel in the heart of the town, over one hundred years old and a place of stories, mysteries and ghosts, at times in splendid isolation during Covid lockdown. The Hydro's links with the town's literary past have given the program a rich resonancy – the historic associations with Henry Lawson, Jim Grahame and Dame Mary Gilmore are a strong foundation to build on. Acknowledgements to Leeton Shire Council, Historic Hydro Management and Western Riverina Arts for their support in establishing the residency and the Historic Hydro Writers Collective – as well as the completion of this book.

Also by Sarah Tiffen and published by Ginninderra Press
Learning Country
Mythica
The Light Breaks Open
The Dark Heart

Sarah Tiffen

Soldier Boy and the Rural Fundamentalists

Vale Les Murray, poet and magnificent human, who passed before this book could be completed. And to all the other dear ones who have been lost this year: deepest sympathies; this is also for them.

Soldier Boy and the Rural Fundamentalists
ISBN 978 1 76109 027 1
Copyright © text Sarah Tiffen 2020

First published 2020 by
GINNINDERRA PRESS
PO Box 3461 Port Adelaide 5015
www.ginninderrapress.com.au

Contents

The Rural Fundamentalists	7
Easter Sunday: an exercise in faith (or Love's Solace)	11
Blood Ties	13
Elegy for a country girl	23
Grand Final 2017	25
Motherlode	30
Tinker, tailor, soldier, spy	35
Whither you go, so I	37
Cantata di Penitenza	40
On the Funeral of the Poet Laureate, the Bard of Bunyah	45
The Separation	53
Child of Mine: thoughts on love and motherhood	56
Instructions From My Father	60
Birthday	66
Sunday Fragments	69
Return to the Sea	70
For Angela Merkel, on the death of Karlov	72
The Infinity Dialogues	75
The Infinity Dialogues II	80
When Shall We Go?	85
New Moon	87
The Valley	88
The summers they dare not speak of, bereft of hope	90
The Rural Fundamentalists II	93
The Rural Fundamentalists III	96
The Rural Fundamentalists IV	98
The Manifesto of a Just Country	101
Breaking the Golden Rule: love in the time of Covid-19	105

The Rural Fundamentalists

We are the Rural Fundamentalists – hear our creed.
Our God is a benevolent God, demanding work
not blood, though sometimes blood is taken,
requiring Sundays for prayer and every other moment for toil,
though sometimes the sky is a purgatory
and sometimes the night is a black hell,
we do not rise up but turn inward.
God of the Seasons, but not of violence –
proselytising sacrifice to ameliorate our own suffering,
assuaging guilt through kindnesses, and ministering calm.
God of Obedience, Acceptance, Common Denominators.
We are the Rural Fundamentalists – hear our creed.

We are the Rural Fundamentalists – hear our prayer.
Steeped deeply in the Deep Ways of Country,
we are not native, but know no other life,
No Other Land – here is where our ancestors lie.
Families born, grown, lived and died, every ritual and loss
every sacred and mundane moment staged and woven here.
How to reckon with whole histories of people bound
to this place, yet but the blink of an eye in the face of millennia?
We cannot, but nevertheless Belong Fiercely and True.
Here time and memory are governed closely. Once we were
   housed in tents.
Time is a sleight of hand. Soon we were our own Kings in
   Grass Castles.
At costs to ourselves and others, melded together
In the one country church.
We are the Rural Fundamentalists – hear our prayer.

We are the Rural Fundamentalists – hear our creed.
Our hearts move in miles and acres, furlongs and inches
and across the arc of sky,
rising at dawn, and folding in with the dark.
Bird call and the lowing of cattle signal changing hours
And with the changing signs of the light we work and move.
Nature has always shaped us, and we asked for nothing but rain.
We make up our own minds, and our own path,
The soil and seasons, our government.
Our currency – water, and light.
We ask for nothing but the right to be unimpeded, free,
with the right to work and spread out. We were settlers. Our benign God led us
and we followed. We came from nothing. And we laboured.
We are the old-fashioned agrarian socialists – egalitarian, self-made,
But bound together.
In the face of the elements, drinkers, poets and brutalists.
We are the Rural Fundamentalists – here we stand.

Here – beyond the reaches of modernity –
held in the Past that is the Future
where the weather and seasons define days and weeks,
learning from birth to listen to cycles of rain,
cycles of sunshine, wind, changes in air, and rhythms of
    planting and growing,
fertile and fallow, the rise and the fall.
Here some Truths are Self-Evident.
Our daily Declarations of Independence.

The human need to grow food, and how this happens –
soil, water, light and seed, farmers' knowledge and toil.
Beyond this, all things are negotiable.
Except honour amongst men.
We are the Rural Fundamentalists – hear our voices
as we take a stand.

We are the Rural Fundamentalists – hear our prayer.
Working to rhythms of seasons, planets and stars –
the midnight watering, the midnight lambing,
the dawn herding, milking and calving,
the sowing before rain, the prayer for clear skies and
the prayer for storms, the silent incantation
for grains fattening, shoots rising, doing deals with the sky
for sunshine, for waylaid frost, for bumper crops,
dry harvest, dry baling, spring lambing, for rain, rain, rain.
And then when the prayers are unanswered, we take stock.
We cultivate a stoic acceptance from our intimate, enforced
entwining capitulation to the Land and Elements.
This, over generations, has turned into
a turn of mind that defines us -
self-worth, self-sufficiency and a breed of nonchalant fatalism:
it is what it is what it is what it is.
Hear our creed. Though some Aberrants fly away in their grief,
And some rail against the fraying light, the vagaries, these
   will be outliers.
Most remain grounded – we have no choice. We are bound
   to the earth and our Place.
We will fight any man, and regulation, that restrains us, or
   threatens our Way of Life.

We are certain and moral. We accept anyone regardless of
   their creed. As long as they
Do the same.

*

We are the Rural Fundamentalists – here we stand.
Our God is an old God, God of seasons, God of growing
pagan and profound, demanding work not blood
though sometimes blood is taken.
Demanding work and humility not vengeance
though sometimes vengeance is necessary.
Though we have guns, we would never turn them to the crowd.
The night is too dark for this, though we may lose ourselves
   at times
amidst the Southern Sky's one billion stars.
Life is too precious to wreak such havoc, and Nature close by.
We are the Rural Fundamentalists – we keep quiet and hold firm,
Cradling one another with a wide stance.

Easter Sunday: an exercise in faith (or Love's Solace)

In the morning, I came from the churchyard slowly,
bearing the burden of your absence like a stone,
awaiting you as always from some moment long ago moment.
The light gave off a burnished hazy sheen.
High up and far across harvest paddocks purging smoke and
dust clouds of white, and red, and trucks rumbling far off.
That easy quiet April roll of industry and grain, and men working
and sunlight like a spilled cup, golden and imbued, the ritual
    and toil.

The sky was blue but strewn, with wisps and streaks,
and off to the east a funnel of pale grey, like a cluster of waves
and darkening slowly, rising low through the air,
while willy-willys tilted and spun, again in red and faded
    white and smoke.

In the heat's mirage, sheep stole on shadowed stilts, stirring
    dust, and dogs
sought shade and languished in a
morning stilled and alloyed,
the sacred bronzed and copper Easter light.

By noon the glaze swung off to the north, and pale and cooler
light opaquely seeped by stealth westward.
The dam trembled, soughing.
A great frenzy of crows, their black murder, rose out of air
discordant and cawing upward from the almond orchard to
    the ragged gums.
Their shadow selves arranged in hieroglyph of beaks and wings.

The gunshot slit the air and all dispersed but two, whose carcasses
swung from askew galah-ravished crowns,
asterisks of bird, exclamatory against blue.

As the afternoon elongated, an elliptical grey stillness ensued.
Easter languor spilled, evoking resurrection and some deep
divinity, in all the gold, the still, the industry, the air, the light.
God deeply present in our wholly human longing and our love.

The dam's surface rilled with airs, while
dogs sat quietly in dirt and sniffed the mud and reedy greens.
Cirrus spread, long canopies of grey, some stormy promise
and I, beset by the nervous grace and wholly human beauty
    of your flesh
that touched me in the holy month and made the holy
    manifest within my body
crucified my heart with softness and in my sleep to rise,
resurrected by love, by you who
was broken, is broken and will break again,
and this light will kiss your body next to mine.
O Love – most perilous of pilgrimages
to healing and redemption, amid comfortless hours of longing.

And then the quiet, quiet dusk that slowly passed into most
    still evening
extolling faith, extolling hope,
my heart assuaged and steady in the dark
awaiting you.

Blood Ties

Later on, the day would become –

one of those pristine days
at the very end of winter
everything kissed and blue
the sun insouciant gold
shining and spilling from the hills
and the sky so deep,
like a blood pulse
and the air so clean and frank
and crystalline.
All elements conspiring
in a murmuring voluptuous beauty –
the Last Perfect Day,
so rich, so lovely, Arthurian, bespoke…

But before, there were omens everywhere
and my body ached before

I woke from nightmares in the predawn,
driven from my bed to flee the house, I

walked through darkling dawn and crypt cold under the
   waned moon,
left the line of orphan gums behind the houses and through
   the underpass,
its cobbled medieval girth full with shadows and
roosting birds,
on to the lake, its sombre mood of grey on grey
and glass, and the russet reeds.

No one stirred.
Fog pushed its implacable folds
against the black silhouette of trees
along the path and out across the
somnolent water, still and silent.
All waiting a signal
to sunder the cloak of greys
from the sun assassin
later to wreak havocs
of gold on the still slumbering land.

There, appeared
a kangaroo in the little wood of silver birch and oaks,
and then with its mate on the water's edge.
It was then just they and I,
and I, heavy with something and fibrillous,
and they, come from the grey fur hills, from the wide expanse
of bush and rivers to the south-west and
up to the Secret Cliff.

Listen and twitch, from their soft felt muzzles and sensual eyes
to the great musculature of their crouch and rise
mythical in that grey light
with only my breath
to accompany them,
as they moved on from the lake to the
palely mottling skies.

But I, I walked on
through fog that took me upside-down
through imaginary winter-bound groves,
lost amongst myself and the hidden land
walking from hidden fears unknown
and thinking of
that arduous night and longer days
that took me toward nothing
in dark dreams – and up the slope and
round the verge
emerging from the fog to still more fog
and scant cars themselves emerging and
re-emerging from fog
their headlights ghostly and searching for home.

And there
in the middle of the wide and silent road
a great kangaroo, fresh-killed and splain
its eyes agog
so silent and so intimate.
It was then just he and I,
and I, heavy with something and fibrillous,
and he, from the wide far hills,
and the Dreaming,
to his great bounding and his fogbound
sudden and silent death,

And there was only
I, the fog and that warm dead thing,
arrested in that moment of recognition and fear,
in our intimate sorrow

O visceral solemnity.

And

I waited
and walked from the verge
into the emptiness
as though stepping out from a great heights into the clouds
and took hold of the sturdy tail
so warm and sinuous, so intimate
and dragged that heavy carcass from the road
avoiding the cars to come
that would scatter its
body in pieces and blood –
and it felt so
heavy and warm though dead,
and sacredly intact
and I – shocked and chastened
bearing witness to that solitary death
stood for a moment,
walked on.

And later the day would become –

one of those brilliant voluptuous days
of light and richness
at the end of a long strange winter
and

*

In the dark I think of omens.

Wondering what would the Old Ones
say of the visit of that
warrior spirit, Kangaroo Warrior spirit
Wambuwany

and it calls to mind
another morning in Another Country

The land of Wiradjuri People –
my land though I am not Wiradjuri but
by place and spirit bound
where the sky is vast and the land
and more ancient in
its vast blood-colours,
where the sky
is the Great Sheltering
and more cerulean, more sweeping and more far –
The Flat Country and the fierce – home of great warrior people.

Here that I ache for when I ache for home,
and the great monolith of the sacred
Bunganbil Mountain, in the
Colinruby Hills
where the spirits call
and sometimes I am afraid,
but always drawn.

I drove through this country one fragile winter dawn
when all the land was sleeping and the sky was bare
and salted with scant stars and the sun coaxed the
horizon but all remained a secret sacrament of mist and
    cobwebs on the land
and the great paddocks all around me – rich, and silent and
    swathed in
the pearling light – it could have been the last day on earth
and only I, the last traveller.

And as I drove I rounded a bend and
up a rise – and again in silent solitude,
and again from the emerging future
two silhouettes of
kangaroos resting on the road,
the black lithograph of their heads
against the sky, as though
languidly reclining and stationary.

And when I drew closer, they still stayed still
and slowly I adjusted to what
I didn't understand, then slowly
perceiving horror –
just they and me in the middle
of the landscape, joined suddenly in some
deep and terrible intimacy.
Mother, and joey –
broken, bleeding and alive
battered on the road and
reaching out to one another
bleating and their eyes beseeching…
their legs were broken and their blood
stained the road as the sun rose,
dead but not dead.

So visceral, so personal
and there was nothing I could do –
but bear witness to them

until a passing truck pulled over
and driver put them down –
it was the only thing to do.

And for a fleeting moment he and I
stood together contemplating Death
and the moral enormity of what we had to do and did.
An act of violence and murder
and an act of honour and grace
that euthanasia
and the blood on my hands as much as his,
but also on the hands of the unknown
traveller who had knocked them down
and thrown the joey from the pouch

and the taste of blood stayed with me
for hours and days.

I still taste the stillness and the sweet cold rush of the air off
    the sleeping land
as the sun drew back the
blankets of the night with her long gold fingers
and bled her light across the paddocks
in a kind of benediction for what we had all done,

and the spirits of the land
offered up the dark secret
through Wambuwany
and I wept
and it seemed like an omen
though I did not know where to put it in
my heart
until

*

That day would become –

one of those perfect days
that I will not forget
for by noon my blood came
dark and heavy, an omen of life and not life
a sacrifice to the Gods,
to keep safe all whom I love above all else
the full moon turned to a perfect half before I knew
and the cycle turned
and I breathed out
and the light was tinged with blood
and even then I accepted that it was
as it should be
no less
no more.

And the blood of the Kangaroo Spirit
became my own
and life
and knowing
and the sun was warm.
And I was glad for this
as my womb bled and my belly was heavy with blood.

*

But sometimes
in the dark
the soughing from the mountain seems so loud
and my dreams are chaotic
and children throng at my feet
and my heart races
and the Warrior Spirit warns me
that storms are rising.

Elegy for a country girl

As spring in its startling zenith turns toward summer
these commonplace but unspeakable types of sadness descend
    upon unnaturally bright days
and break all before them, wave upon wave.
The heart wavers.
There is no consolation.

Oh, beautiful child, wilful and bright beyond bearing,
who suddenly decreed the world too fierce,
too frightening and difficult to carry her, to keep her here,
and so left it in a violent flash,
an act too awful, too unequivocal to dare, yet dared and done.

Surely you could not have known that in that doing
you would send unending waves of darkness through the
hearts of all who loved you and were loved by you, forever
    scarred.
To bestow on all beloveds that. Great. Weight. Forever more.

Oh, beautiful girl, you were too young to know how much
    you're needed here –
how much sunlight, how much goodness and honey you fed
    to the ecosystem of your bright life.
Forever mourned for leaving the whole world who needed
    you to live.

Poor darling girl – you could not see how utterly enough you
    were and would have been,
in all your bright majesty, your queenly power and divine light.
Forever now enshrined in that moment of purposeful leaving,
a halo of golden tragedy about your perfect, hard-perfected self.

And now your hurt and your pain inscribed on every heart,
    tattooed, branded, burned –
the ones who bore you, who followed you, who wished you
    joy, who cherished you, who came
and tried so very, very hard to save you, those who gave you
    life and willed you life.
And yet you turned away.

Now, now, now into the ever-repeating moments of the
    future as it becomes the anguished
past. Unspeakable. Unspeakable.
And so foreshadowing every grief that will ensue – unquiet,
    dark and restless grief,
unending sadness and the shaking of all knowing and all belief.

The world was not enough for you,
though how deeply did all who knew you know you were, for it,
more than enough.
Enough.
Enough.
Enough.

Coda

We see you in the golden light of dying days, a shadow just
    beyond our reach,
an echo of a voice a laugh, in half a dream and nightmare,
    eyes squinting into the sun,
almost there. Enough.

Grand Final 2017

when by one point, the Mighty Phantoms claimed back the Rugby Union
Premiership Crown and reigned again as kings of the Southern Inland
(with acknowledgement to Seamus Heaney and all Irish kings and poets)

O Glorious Day of Victory, after the glorious fight,
and the Boys were *Back*!

And then, that night after the Game –
the streets alight with torches and horns,
and the pub awash with beer, and a joyous madness
as the whole town turned out to celebrate the Big Win –
half a century they'd waited for this.
From the Battlefield of Number One Oval to the Temple of
    the Wade Hotel –
jubilant rambling in raucous clusters, the sweaty cheers, the
    body heat
and rallying and drinking in mad, joyous rage.

'The Premiership!' they cried and hugged one another and laughed
and wiped their tears and held each other tight,
slapped backs with big hands that had lately
downed tools, rough and smelling of dirt and grease –
now with beer, now with the rough hug and the cheer.
Blood brothers were they, never broken or disbanded,
bold and wild, and strong and close, their stout proud hearts
    and their
dreams intermingled, and the love and loss of small towns
and the secrets they all shared.

And the Honorary Mayor of the small town moved amongst them,
Quiet King, High Priest of the Phantom Temple and the
    Order of Purple Men,

walked among revellers and warriors,
calm amongst them, he moved from group to group amidst
    the throng
bestowing words and raffle tickets, praise and yarns upon them,
and ministering to his people,
as the singing and drinking rose to a roar
and the jubilant tribesmen chanted and sang the Songs of Old,
so he walked through the room full of the life of men and beer,
full of the mad vigour of victory
and he seemed amongst them to be both shepherd and lamb,
And basking in it – from the sticky floorboards to the rafters,
And looked happy that his work was done.

And then, to the deafening beery summit, on the Top of the
    Known World,
when the noise rose to a roar, and they chanted the Victory Song
And recounted the Stories of Old, and it was Grand and Beautiful
And his eyes shone with it, though he did not smile until later –
when the Islander Men climbed the pulpit of the pub stage
And held the cup aloft, and right there, where they were
    gathered and thronging,
they sang a spiritual from Pacific Lands in Pacific tongue,
    moving and in dreams,
and their voices all in harmony upon the thronging stage,
aching and beautiful and languid as frangipani, rich and sweet
and all were awash with the drunken love,
their hearts burst to overflowing with pride and glee,
and then were his eyes shining from a fire within, and from love –

And the whole town was the World in that moment, and the
   World was
Gloriously United, and the Islanders and the Celts were one, and
all amongst them, he stood, both joyous and becalmed, and sure
that he'd given them everything he had, and more, and sure
that this victory would last a thousand years, and spur the
   kings and poets to
acclaim the blessed day forever more, and he was glad –
though too was the Cloak of Sadness upon him like an
   armour and in fact it was
only the courage and love of men that sustained him so he
   would not fall,
and all burned with the Miracle of the One Point.

And so the night went on, a battle cry, a victory dance, a melee –
a stand against struggle, a defiance, a heart song and a hymn.
And feel – reverberating, that deep camaraderie, that
   brotherly love as
tangent and tangible as divine light, and
illuminating all who stood amongst it, and himself, lit up,
his mouth in a half-smile and his eyes alight but tinged also
   with fatigue,
and those who watched him might perceive also that he bore
the great and quiet burden of his work.
For it was he, who stood amongst them and as one of them,
who in all other times was called upon to heal and save them,
to rescue them from themselves, from revelry and recklessness,
after follies and fates – in dark hours and in the beautiful days –

he it was who must be the witness bearer, and the saviour
in small moments and the great tragedies, on the dark
roads, and in their beds, the accidents and violences, quiet
    passings and quick
births, in the factories and out on lonely farms, in lanes and
    streets where
lately they had lived, and where – in a moment –
they might be reduced to become
something other than themselves – reduced to brokenness of
    bodies, or of hearts – and
he, always vigilant, always ready, and carrying this knowledge
    like a cross,
and it was two parts love and one part fear that drove him,
    and in all that,
the deep need for the great tide of men and victory
and to move amongst them, loving them and knowing he
    had made them live,
and may again, and how quietly he carried the burden of that
    duty
and tried so hard to save them every single time he could,
but bore also at all times the shadow of grief and sorrow, and
carried deep within him the souls of children who were lost,
including his own – the littlest angel – the lost, the lost –
and how the unbearable pain of her small absence was forever
    stored in him
and shaped him – (even now in the wild brilliance of this night)
– the loss that never passes, even while her spirit
flourishes in the wild Irish hearts of the living children, and
    lives in them, and

in his heart, and oh, how he hoped his own heart was strong
 enough to bear
this, and that he too may lay down when the storm has passed,
to tend his own weariness and to be loved and rest,
and be restored to God and to himself.
And all this was in his face and in the carriage of his body in
 the crowd.

And yea – the Tribe of Phantom Men grew louder in their
 revelry – and wild
And sang of that Grand Final that will never be forgotten,
And that one point victory, that joy, and they knew, that
 legends would be
told of that glorious day and the gallant men who brought it
 home
and all the men who came before – and all who came after –
and the generations to come would remember, and for that
 moment
Nothing. Else. Mattered.
but the glory of that win, that glorious Grand Final,
when by One Point, the Mighty Phantoms claimed back the
 Crown of Rugby Union and
reigned again as Kings of the Southern Inland.

*

And he smiled at his Old Father who was proud,
and later laid down in his secret cave and dreamed –
the Cup on the Mantel, and the spirits of Ancients,
promising succour, love and strength in the coming days.

Motherlode

We drove along the highway, she sleeping, me thinking
and listening to radio talk, stories of war, stories of flood, and
   loving her,
and then she woke and we rattled on,
dodging the time before us, talking of people and gossip,
theories, and nothing, listened to music.
Trucks thundered past, and sandstone ravines, and then Sydney,
oiled and sinuous in afternoon light, full of memory and conspiracy.

Our room looked over the ocean –
Beach View, a statement of absolute fact.
Beach and water languidly fine,
the air a consulate warmth,
balmy and soporific.
We held hands, chattered,
Went and sat in the beauty parlour
on humming chairs and got our toenails painted
amid the matrons and tanned schoolgirls.
The languid Friday evening rhythm of a beach suburb,
always at ease.
Groups of Islander boys, little children and couples
wandering the promenade,
walkers and surfers, the murmur of the sea,
And a breeze like a tropical salve
this far north.

Hungry and lazy, we ordered seafood,
and gobbled it, chatting on the balcony
as the sunset settled in watercolours, bathing the bay
in rose and the water a still blue green,
And the Friday night buzz arose from down on the street.

Later, as she was resting I called her 'Look, baby' and
we peered through glass at the looming peerless moon who
spilled her milky essence to ripple on the dark sea, and above –
planes' industrious ant lights scribbling the bitten rind of
   night sky.
'That will be you,' I said.
Soon she slept.
I pushed our beds together and held her warm hand
as I too fell asleep later, fitfully,
the city moving below and around us in its
strange nightly rhythms – the jubilance, leisure and violence
   in waves,
the tailing off of laughter in the dark. Oh Sydney, citadel of
   thieves and whores, bootleggers
and scoundrels, dealing and wheeling and scrapping in your
   unending dirty broken glory.

In the morning, nervous and bright, we walked the coast
   path up and down
amidst joggers and dog walkers, watching
sea swimmers and the shoals of surfers in wetsuits
out on the bombora below the headland.
We sought the shore, a moment of stillness amid the tide
   bearing us on –
'34 minutes to the airport, via Botany Road'
through dusty, immigrant parts of the old city to our last hour
before a separation longer than any since she left my body.

Oh, the airport was all humanity –
people coming and departing from all the globe's corners –
waiting and moving and watching in waves and throngs as
    the clock stole our minutes.
At the departure gate, I held her head to my chest,
and absorbed her presence just like many years before when
    she was three
and we rocked together on an old chair in the back winter
    garden,
her little curly head in the crook of my neck –
then and now'
'I love you. Love, Love, Love!"
The last photo, the last glance, the backward smile,
and love's dark flower filled my chest – and deep in
my stomach, my solar plexus – as I let her go.

*

Soon, to the tunnel and the highway, heading south to the
    dark and cold.
As far and fast as I dared as the wind rose and I moved in
    stealth or in a dream
silent and baffling, to another place, another Universe where
    the sky fell in sheets of grey
upon undulating staccato land.
And at last came I to the Kingdom of Lake St George.
Oh, mythical landscape of spirits carved from eons through
    which I must pass
to leave the body blow of parting behind me – and make it
    home alive.

The vast immutable knuckle of the hills,
a prone sleeping giant dismantling and folding the earth as a blanket –
clasped in the escarpment and presiding over the mist-ridden flats of the mythical lake.
Far off, red cows – Hereford – sleek as butter, grazing on the lake bed,
and further pebble pockets of sheep, clustered cloistered out amidst yellow foamy ground.
And the Grand Angus – their regal black sheen – seemed walking on water,
great beasts suspended on a lake surface there and not there.
Mysterious in fissures the greens and the greens away and the heavy brown
and the looming mist of rain and dark, dark, dark, in ancient memory.
Fences like stitches in the lake's time, bent and bespoke at intervals, the mist.
The falling world felled upside down and gaunt
trees and rain like falling silver spears and spirits, and the black sky, and the
slants of preternatural gold sun relinquished from the cloudbank.
And further out again, fantastical mountains arraigned with the white marvel
of the Great Medieval Turbines turning silently against a pearl sky.
All this at once as I drove and the dark fell, and the snow, a heartbeat
from shaping out of the brooding rock and leaden closing night.

And she – she in the sky, soon in Finland, soon again in
London – back to the Mother Country on her beautiful
   pilgrimage.
A goddess and a child – Mine! Mine! – Loved beyond word
and unleashed on the golden thronging world
to shape herself in the golden light of history
and Europe's lavish incredulous monuments – its darkness
   and joys.
My heart – a crucible of keening love – the motherlode of
   fear, unending joy.

Tinker, tailor, soldier, spy

(for Soldier Boy)

Inscrutable quiet man, carefully stepping amidst chaoses of small making,
storyteller and heart minder,
broker and tidier of broken and untidy lives,
Father Spirit looms in you
as you mindfully tread and move in contained grace
among the long wide undulating structures of the day,
the sleep that eludes you etched on your beautiful face.
Built for fighting, with a fighter's muscular grace, the violence casually contained beneath your skin,
how you carefully, carefully held me
when you laid me down and stroked my skin in long, slow currents
like a deep river, and barely touched and slid amongst my rushes and pools
like a priest making sacrament on altars of trembling flesh,
like an otter in cool green waters.
How you carry stillness like a battle wound, the heavy burden of your role,
how you watch and think, how you wait, how you say little amidst storms.
Catholic courage, Soldier Boy, take heart. How you grapple and wrangle yourself,
how you speak plainly and take me
with purposeful desire until I melt into you
and give myself away unto you.
You
walk like a spy, an undercover operative through the

long exhaustion of days, the sleepless nights
and the dreams of precipices and walks with your
mother in the red rose garden asking me to hold
the child within the man, poised for flight.
Submission is a gift
I offer you, and you receive with eyes wide open, I
turn to liquid and spill upon you like a river.

Whither you go, so I

I will –
lay you down upon the surface of
the glassy evening river
and let you float with your eyes closed
like a cross until the fishes come and nibble at your toes
and birds nest in your hair and flowers are strewn on the
    ripples of the water
rippling from your heart beating strong and slow,
and tine dragonflies alight on the trembling reeds
as I am trembling
in the magic summer of the evening's river
washed with the last gold of the day,
and when you are done
I will pull you slowly shoreward
with a rope of silk and tears.

I will –
Lay you down on the clean white sheets
of the soft bed, face down and unbroken
and touch your skin, so slowly
from your ears to your back, from your arms
to your fingers
with the lightest touch, over and over and down your legs
and feet, and stroke you quietly in the cool air, as the fan
    caresses us
and the room,
and gently stroke with the tips of my fingers
on all the scars and wounds of the years
until all the grief and all the fear is gone from the cells
of your muscle and bone, and take a cloth of
softest flannel and wash you clean with cool water

until you feel reborn and
the tangle in your head
dissipates into the light
and, like a child, all the tears
flow from you until you are spent,
until all your anger is undone.

And I will –
say no word, but lay down slowly
by your side, and curl into you
and sleep so quietly without moving
breathing so lightly – and cover us both
with a soft blanket and feel your warmth
and breath, and know the even fall of your breath
and rise, and wait in peace, in patience
for the storms to subside and wash away
and the dawn to rise over the bush
in a cool green hush
and we will wake in grace
and open our eyes to the stillness
and smile.

And I will –
sit beside you quietly
and hold your hand while you speak your
sorrow and bewilderment away and
listen calmly as you rage,
and bear witness to all calamity
and pain, until it too subsides
and you learn to breathe again
and then I will submit to you gently

and take your body into mine and hold it there
and never cry out and never wonder,
aut open to you and feel the awakening of hope
and tremble as you breathe yourself alive again
anto me, and rise, ready to be forgiven,
ready for redemption – for restitution.

And all your enterprises
will be sacrosanct and treasured, and your
dreams will turn from loss, and your
darkness fall away
and your heart be healed, and mine
and we can build something
small and clean-lined, and I will
work beside you and we will build a
summer house of wood and stone
and all the animals will come to marvel
at the plainness and simplicity of joy,
and feel the gentle flow of light that suddenly
irradiates your heart
and

then we would laugh
because the reason was never clear
but the meaning is apparent
and you might see
the stillness in your mind
reflected in the sky,
and be at peace.

as I.

Cantata di Penitenza

Dream Fragments

in my dream the light is rising
green amassing and the dark falling
and the clouds a riot of bruises and storm
and crawling molecules of ozone fill the air
I see I am toiling against a tide
and it is very hard
and suddenly I find myself on cliffs
that turn into a precipice
high up against mountains
rocky, sharp and vertiginous and
I'm terrified fighting against the wind
battling against the gale…

and in my dream
I'm at a room in a forest
and it's winter
and the fire is crackling
and there are people thronging
their hubbub bubbles in my ear
and I'm searching
and see you and we meet in the middle of the room
and we hold each other
we feel so relieved.

I wake and long for you.

Maybe

Maybe the night is just too long, and dark
Maybe the fear is the ballast for everything you do
Maybe your longing is too much, maybe the pain too much
Maybe too scared of what might come,
Maybe the time too raw, the heart too ragged,
The feeling too much, the weight too heavy,
The feeling the doubt too strong
Maybe fears lurking below the surface
Maybe ready to burst
Maybe too deep and dark
The tangle, the hurt too hard to shake
Maybe too far, maybe too close
Maybe heartbroken and spent,
Maybe the fire is burning already
Maybe too sweet, maybe too far to resist,
Maybe worth the chance, what may be.

Faltering

That yawning chasm of dark pain that cradles us
unbearably sweet and fierce
flinging us down to the rocky naked ground
on our knees and bleeding, on our knees with grief, asking
what is there to be done, what is there to be done?
Paralysed and fearful
and only truth telling is left to do in the ensuing silence.
Only truth telling.
Where to from here?
Love and fear.
Love and fear.

Winter breaking

Winter broke on a Sunday
And some spring hope broke through
When the sky stopped resisting and split with blue,
And trees relented and moved in gentle grace in the light
And the sun, the sun – let go and spoke majestic yellow of times to come,
Coaxing the world, coaxing birds and shoots to alight, coaxing the world
From its long hidden hours, its dark secrets into beautiful equating green
And switching life – currawongs, magpies, wattlebirds, wrens – filling the
Unnatural golden afternoon, with the testing calls and twitches, the hopesong
Of winter passing, yielding, releasing us into the light.
And I slept in the yard inflecting that wild honey light drinking it into my skin
The warm liquor of a life coming undone and open
Slake my skin, slake me, slake my heart,
And felt you out there in the world,
As scared and gentle and human as one could ever be,
And sweetly, sweetly coming to me.

The Undertow

Giant shifted under the mountain dark,
spilled gold from the cover of his cloud cloak
like God's hand.
Waiting in my home crucible for your alchemy.
Moon Huntress push her sharp glow through
velvet night masks, streaking, I delve
down down to the subterranean truth of your
dark glow
all go,
down down to the hungry undertow
to the yearning undertow
just to see your face in the
maleficent furnace of this land
you fine hand on my breast milking
tears for you, silence and the hard shine of your blue eye
Lullaby Baby
Going down
to dream on the river bed
to the deep down undertow
to drown for you, surrender to the currents of your
deep down dark love undertow.

On the Funeral of the Poet Laureate, the Bard of Bunyah

And so now has the funeral ended as the day battens down to winter storms
and trees thrash against the air.
I imagine that small church in the hills, up the bush track potholed with a century of hooves and wheels.
Ferns and bracken flocking at the track's edge, the mysterious camouflages of light and green
and pale bark and lizards' flick, and the long tall shadows of mountain ash.
The honour guard – marking the pilgrimage to your great passing.
And where do I put this yawning loss,
this loss that is nothing less than the immeasurable?
And where do I put my grief on this wintery afternoon,
so sombre, and such sombre mood bespeaking sombre, sacred thoughts?
Only in silent vigil it seems for all words are now diminished, Dear One.
It seems impossible that you are stilled, and this immense, impossible silence ensuing from
your loss.
Surely you are there at the altar smiling, thinking of more thoughts to conjure
into words like knitted spiderwebs, handcrafted miniatures, or diamonds
fossicked from your wildly mythic mind?
But no, they say, they say that you have gone, the funeral,
it's the funeral of the Poet Laureate – they tell us so.
And it must be.

I picture all of them, the townsfolk, they are your people –
   farmers, woodcutters, shopkeepers, cottage craftsmen and
   women, humble men and women, dairymen, blacksmiths,
   foresters, dogs and scruffy children, all in silence.
Crowding the pews, they are, silently spilling down the aisle,
   the steps, filling the alcove and sprawling
out over the ramshackle bush lawn,
the whole congregation, the great Catholic diaspora
   composed in a
silent, breathing, collective homage.
And before them all, the huge coffin bedecked with flowers,
buttressed to house your colossal mortal frame, but barely
   containable
colossal heart.
Here they all stand in tribute to you,
familiar and beloved, beloved returned, not shunned, not
   stunted or debrided now
with scorn, but wholly theirs, the biggest crowd Saint
   Bernadette's Catholic Church in
Krambach ever saw! Nor ever will again.
They circle you and bring you home
as one of them, the broken boy inside the giant man,
you, Cecil's boy, who alone turned their lives into poetry
   without an ounce of artifice.
Oh, how you keenly saw and deeply loved each one, each full
   of grace
And here they stand – eyes wet and hats in hands.

*

And so, without grand gestures, has stilled the great unquiet mind.
And in the noonday silence, how the axe has fallen one last time
upon you, and the ancient craft of thoughts that fell from you,
you left in such a commonplace and quietly human way,
but surely you would revel in the shockwave that reverberates
 around
your absent self, now held within the ground
And you spoke only of great love, take solace in that love
of man and animal and all your dreams and deities, your vision
kith and kin,
that absolves you of all sin.
Rest easy, man,
though the chatterers all have their say – I laugh to think of you
appraising and abrading them – Oh agitator, they proclaim,
Oh contrarian, Oh posturer for redneck humble folk and
 working men,
postulant for ancient rural egalitarianism – hillbilly, miscreant,
 inbred, autist,
lefty-righty – nothing but yourself –
Poverty mythologiser, Christian apologist or apostate,
 simpleton, bumpkin, genius
Blah, blah – or those who sought to exile you now getting
 kudos and limelight from
pontificating about your greatness, but only in reference to
 their own, Oh how you would
slyly chuckle in your toothy guileless way
to see them flung in mimicries of intellect
while they completely miss the point in death in life of your
 majestic, quintessential outside inside view,

your sturdy giant fingers always nimbly on the pulse of our
    original, unnoticed, and half-forgotten truths
    memorialised and anthologised through you –

*

And how your grief and wildness played out
a thousandfold in filigrees of love and deepest darkest sense –
the milking stool, the bed, the land, the forest and the people
    there
and still the sweet and woody unpeopled air,
the boot, the axe, the table top, the cows who nuzzle at the
    fence,
lonely rural miles and immigrants and shy smiles, socialist
    and anarchist
the sweet land and the water and the hills:
a truth too simple and yet too immense
for us to grasp, too hurried to take pause and see ourselves
in subhuman redneck weatherboard cathedrals,
and yet you offered it in great grace, a great map of ourselves
from out your mind to follow in until we reach the
hallowed ground of comprehension.
And see, you knew that you had left this treasure to us all,
and so, you left so ordinarily and quiet,
and would have revelled, slyly, chucklingly
in the sudden realisation that has now reverberated round
your absent self.

*

Rest easy, Great Man.
No more worry, no more grief
no more fear that pecked so darkly at you
and without relief.
No more stoushes, battlers' battles, life's defeats
accusations of curmudgeonliness, anti-establishment,
anti-intellectual elites – the labelling of your true ungoverned
 heart.
No more this, and that – subhuman redneck flaws, etc.
Shut up the book, lay down your mighty pen, lay down your
 great colossal body to the ages,
eschew the fearful tyranny of hate.
No more tea.
No more gossip.
No more awkward earnest audiences with the Queen.
No more whisky chat by the roaring fireside, no more
 Dreaming Tree.
No more beers in Romano's courtyard, no more driving in
 the dark
or on the winding road in the land of blood and honey,
no more paddock bashing, no more Angus cattle on the Lachlan.
Just silence.
And your poetry.

Oh you, who were so kind to give me succour in the dark,
 and who lit the spark.

Stop the clocks
He's dead. He's dead.
The greatest living poet now is gone.
Pack up the moon, dismantle the sun, pour away the ocean,
sweep up all the wood,
for nothing now can ever come to any good.
But yet your words – dear man – your words bequeathed,
the great monument to your great mind
left for us mere mortals to covet, relish, and hold dear
the story that you told us of ourselves will carry on
in all the small and sacred moments of a life.
Five children and a wife behind,
and no more overhung by childhood's
overarching tragedy that shaped you to the man
who showed us all the things we should not be,
and all those magically
we are
we can.

With acknowledgements to W.H. Auden, 'Funeral Blues'

The Separation
(for Tom)

I went with my first born to the airport,
and it was full of all humanity in transit, thronging.
It seemed that the Whole World was there, in that place -
people everywhere from Everywhere, colours and voices
 folding into a
chaos of leaving and coming, holding each other, and letting
 each other go.
And here I am amongst it with my one. My Son. Oh, darling
 child of mine.
Older now than when I carried him into the world,
but still so young, so fresh and nervous, so bright and brave.
A boy, a man, my child.
He and his boyhood friend about to see the world.
To leave. I tried to understand it; but could not.

*

In the motel room the night before, staring at the ceiling
 while the two boys slept–
I had conceived a plan – to write the Right Words on paper
to fold into a little square of hope and love and place inside
 his pocket
on parting. My Son. For him to carry like a talisman as he
 flew a thousand miles from me.
But what is there to say? What words could be enough? For this?
You came into this world because I loved you before you were
 made and given
from the Beginning beyond Beginnings, and I loved the World
and gave you to it, to live and grow and laugh and learn, to
 fill the world

and my heart with love, and yours,
to drink in everything there is – all the joy and wonder that there is.
To take it all.
It was always for this. And all the dreams that have brought us here.
We have prepared for this a thousand times – the long labour and the sudden birth,
the utter love and fear, the leavings with your father, to school, to visit the farm
on the long holidays with Grandma and Papa,
your football triumphs, your dark days, your adventures, each parting
I now see was a preparation for this moment
For Love is but a series of sacred separations
and so
I can only let you go, as that is how it's meant to be –
with all my prayers and all my love tucked in the pocket of your heart.
And the only words that ever saw a child set forth upon the world:
'Go well, my darling, be brave, be safe, be true. Take my love,
for now, for while you are away, for while you travel
and for when you soon return.
Go well, remember courage and wonder in all things.'
My son. So beautiful and strong.
So true of heart, my all.

I hold him close and let him go,
Like the first parting and the last – it is impossible,
    inevitable, and utter.
And watch as he is swallowed by the sea of all Humanity,
and I turn back to home, to wait,
preparing only for his return.

Child of Mine: thoughts on love and motherhood

(for Wilbur)

I remember in my dreams having to learn to allow you to fly,
    letting go
Even as I got used to you always being in my sideview, beside
    me, on my hip,
tucked in the big bed with me, a small sleeping angel, while
    we weathered unthinkable
storms, even then, it was unthinkable to let you go.
Even at the first, when the time came for labour, we resisted it.
I planted roses in the front garden as a storm front rolled in,
    and the wind rose, and the sky
blackened as contractions began, it was time, but I wanted to
    keep you safe with me.
Two days of labouring, and still I was in awe when you
    arrived, and looked at me as though
we had always known each other.
I told the midwife I wanted to keep the placenta and I took it
    home with us
to the house in Woralul and kept it in the freezer until I had
    the strength to garden again,
and then one day I took it out to the backyard and buried it
    beneath the tree –
And they told me that Italian folklore says
that the child whose placenta is in the garden will never stray
    too far from home,
and even then, I had to hold you and learn to let you go
and even now, I will always be needing to allow you to fly,
and even now I will always be holding you for
you are too much a part of me to ever let you go.

*

Even before I knew it was you, you were beside me.
We were connected even before I was born.
You arrived and looked at me, fully formed and
recognising me even before I had time to comprehend what
 had occurred –
seriously appraising me in our shared raw state.
The familiar feeling of your skin against me, even though we
 had only just met.
You came to me with purpose
guiding me forward to the whole.
All the days of trouble and joy you lay beside me quietly,
rode on my hip from the bed to the kitchen, kitchen to car,
all through the busy sweet days and long weeks, a
quiet companion while we rode out the storms
binding us all in with your small serious presence.
How you watched the pantomime of days
at the end of each stretch checking that I was collected
from fray to fray.
Your little feet on the stairs, bringing me tea in the morning,
Thinking deep thoughts in the recess of difficult days
Sitting with turtles and frogs, sitting with dogs in peace
Pushing me to be better.
Patient beyond your years.
Bearing witness, always taking stock, being kind.
Even before I knew it was you, you were always beside me.
The better part of me in all things

*

Motherhood is my great reckoning, nothing matters more,
    my flesh and blood enlisted
in the unceasing acts of LOVE that are as fundamental as air.
    I would
die for you a thousand times, though
in truth I have failed you and rallied, and failed you and
    rallied and
failed you and needed you a thousand times over.
While the world raged, we were we, you, steady and there.
I have missed you every moment we have ever been apart.
It will always be this way.
It will never change, the slight tension in my breath and my
    skin
until I am with you again.
I will miss you every day we are apart, though separations
    compound.
In my dreams, I am reaching for you, even after we have
    talked three
times on the phone that day.
If I was half the person you are in your strong quiet heart I
    would feel
worthy, though worthiness fails me, the human frailty I
    battle.
Motherhood, the great reckoning.

*

I recall us sitting at the dining table at Yarran St. Those
    difficult and wholesome days
where I almost fell into the abyss, where only my children
    saved me.
You would say 'Let your life unfold,' after telling us about the
    Thinking Club you
and your friends had made at school.
'And what do you do in the Thinking Club?' I'd ask.
'Sit on the log and think about things,' you'd say in earnest.
Now, it is you that won't allow us to falter, insisting on order,
reflecting on chaos, forgiving, even while you hold us to
    account.
It is you now, grown as you are, and the world so uncertain
    and wild
who cautions against haste, who reminds me to be strong,
    who does not
allow one inch of delusional thinking. 'Be rational, Mumma,'
    you say.
I am only me because of you.
I try to be, though motherhood is two parts love to one part
    fear,
And the rationale for any parting is never clear.

Instructions From My Father
(on his birthday)

The two years since the Great Grand Party
have taken their toll in small
imperceptible steps, more tracking thoughts of worry
across your busy mind, more contours of fatigue on your long frame,
the nicks and bruises on your arms and legs from your labours –
the trees you prune, the wire you cut and bend, fastening fences,
twisting gate clasps, chains and locks and posts and chocks,
the tools and chores and battles of your work,
and your routines.
A natural progression that you like to ignore, downplay, and
Press On Regardless – a noble creed.
It is the way to Get Things Done.
But now more settled in your resolve to persevere, and a
gentler resignation to the things, despite your great unending efforts,
you cannot change, that things and people will just be the way they are.
Your practical disposition, hard-headed and clear-sighted in many things, but
emotional and stubborn in the simple matters of your irrational heart,
dogged and loyal to the point of blind to the principles of family that formed you.
Father.
On the morning of your 82nd birthday,
the April light is a dry and burnished gold
as a painting painted in impressionistic autumn hues,

Reds and browns, purples and mustards of an older age,
medieval, colonial, as though the landscape is just an old
 master brought out from the shed,
and brushed off, with the sheen of webs and dust still hanging.

In a quiet moment between breakfast and the long late lunch
 of family egos and deep
conflictual intents, we do the rounds.

Here is the pump at the rainwater tanks by the back door, for
 house water.
Flick the trip switch if the pressure goes, call Glenn Heath
 with any issues, should anything go awry.
Here are the ten young cattle roans and blacks clustered in
 the house paddock
by the peppercorns and under the signal gum were the shape
 of a bark canoe still scars the great trunk. They'll be right,
 they can wander, graze the lucerne,
and make their way to the back dam with the willows
 weeping and the fat grass on the channel banks. All they
 have to do is stay alive, and fatten.
Just count them every day – still ten? That's all you have to do.
Feed the chooks in the morning and let them out to fossick
 in the afternoon. Thirteen, count them when they go back
 in at dusk.
But keep the gates shut to the garden, or they will busily
 unearth all bulbs, all daisies and geraniums, though the soil
 does need a good scratch and fat worms will please them.

Don't. Forget. To Shut. Them Up – they will follow you into
    the chook pen, just call them with wheat.
There is a fox around, we saw it in the paddock two days ago.
More than one, I think, and feral cats, and Walshy fighting
    off the foxes from the lambs.
And
if you walk in the chook pen, don't walk the dirt into the
    house! No, Dad, I know we don't do that, I grew up here
    you know.
He says it twice more, and puts a note on the fridge to the
    same effect.
DON'T WALK CHOOK SHIT IN THE HOUSE!
Our bedroom door stays shut. No one needs to go in there.
    Yes, Dad.

Come on now, let's go over to the dam, and check the water
    pump, so you know how to put
the sprinklers on.

The dam is cool and green, cleaned by alum and weeded in
    the way Dad does, walking through the water chest deep
    pulling up the weeds by the root.
Reflections of the blue hazy sky, the gracious ragged gums,
    the wisps of high cloud.
Across the water I heard mewling, feral cats appeared from
    the pump house, half-grown, mangey, stringy mutts. He
    can't hear them because he hasn't got his hearing aids on –
    but their little scratchy calls are tinsel on the wind, and I
    tell him – there's kittens there.
'Well, we'll have to do something about them, wont we?' he says.
I don't want to know.

And wait while he goes back to the house, with the puppy on his lead, listening to the soporific sound of the insouciant April morning, bucolic still and all the lazy droning sound of small life – insects, birds, bees, crickets, frogs – the tiny web of it all in symphony.

He's gone for ages.

He comes back later with the shotgun, and goes into the pump house while I look away.

Two down, and one black ugly thing that gets away. Done. Just what needs to happen.

Now – here's the timer. Here is the switch. If the pressure goes, twist this off, and turn this tap and pump water up out of the valve until all the air bubbles are gone. Turn it off. Easy.

Turn the sprinklers on every second night, it should be enough.

A lifetime of water vigilance – that deep intrinsic knowledge in the rituals of pump, pipe, hose, stops, channels, bailiffs, sprinklers, gauges.

That is the lore of this place – and no one has more reverence for water than an irrigator, steeped in this management for all his life.

Water grows food, gives life, makes dry things green. Water makes oranges, rice, cherries, tomatoes, peaches, plums, potatoes, lemons, grapes – and everything else grown here. Poultry, cotton, cows, sheep, horses, almonds, everything.

There is nothing he does not know about the ebb and flow.

I write it all down in my notebook.

Flood the fruit trees – quinces, pears, apples, cherries, olives – don't let them get thirsty.

And here's the other pipe – that services the little citrus row.

They don't look well. I don't know, he says, they keep
   dying on me.
Just keep the water up to them, and all along the drive, every
   second day, keep them watered, and the other trees around
   the tennis court – the second tap, the hose, at least once
   every three days.
And the grand old navel tree by the back door, that has
   furnished us with great globes of jewelled oranges every
   winter of my life – keep it watered – watch if the leaves
   start to curl,
And the lemon tree (lavish and bounteous) beside it – lemons
   as big as melons and laden with juice – keep it watered too.
The guns are locked away and the key is hidden. The garage
   is locked – just to be sure to keep the Monaro safe – its
   prize vintage shiny red glory.
And here is the key to the blue ute – but lock the cars at
   night, some vagabonds and thieves, we're on the corner
   and you never know.
(some night later a fracas on the corner in the night proved
   his point)

What a steady, peaceful way to spend the morning, and
   following you round, I feel that companionable lull
   learning, taking notes.
Father.
I want to learn how to be as stoic, as practical, as
   clear-headed as you can be.
How to prove myself worthy, how to be careful and strong,
   how to work hard

with all my being, to reabsorb the routines of the day into my own rhythms, how to honour your legacy and hold it in good stead.

And how to be brave, while feeling fear – as we look ahead to weather such storms as will beset us soon enough.

Happy Birthday, Dad.

Birthday

(for my grandmother on 10 January 2017)

Today it is your birthday.
Today you were born one hundred years ago.
Today I honour your small brown hands
and quick brown eyes,
your small body busy in the kitchen
calming and oiling the conversation with wise, bright words.
Lamingtons and tea in the afternoon,
toast and tomato for dinner,
and your laugh, ready, and your chatter.
Your red lipstick and gold watch and thin bones.
Your busy order and neat shoes.
Your stories from long ago,
and your kind heart, like a small bird
tending us and the small world about us
with a stoic and practical pride.
You dismissed with a laugh and a psssht
our grandfather's persistent cantankerous mockery,
his belittling, and smirking, smoking in the kitchen
gripping the pipe between teeth,
between white knuckles, shiny stretched skin.
You bore his post-war struggle.
You were sunny in the shadow of his anger.
I deeply honour how we found you, after his funeral,
weeping in the dark, surrounded by his clothes
watched over by his portrait in air force uniform,
his medals. And his fierce abrasive intellect
bestowed upon his children like a mark.

I recall small details, small moments–
your quiet decline, your peaceful bewildered relinquishing of life.
I told you in that golden afternoon 'It's OK to go', as you lay curled like a small child on the big bed with a shaft of light at your back, watching something in the middle distance, murmuring.
I think you heard me, 'You can let go.' Was that all right?

Oh and now the years of silence, the grief that has become part of me.
You are there in the brown eyes of my children,
my daughter's sensible practical industry.
You come to me in dreams and give me gentle advice when I feel lost.
And how your hands have become my mother's hands, your daughter,
And mine hers, her daughter…and sometimes
I feel a strange confusion at your absence,
as though just round the corner, or after 3 p.m.,
you will appear and we will continue as before,
and that it was not real to see you lying, but only sleeping
and that it was only yesterday that I brushed your hair
and held your hand,
and laughed,
and all the years reduced to this moment,
a moment, on your 100th birthday.
More love with passing years not less.
Your absence – impossible to understand, the tears possess.

Sunday Fragments

Sunday I

Sunday near the ocean at year's end,
always cool and quiet
green waves, white sand, grey sky.
Gulls, one, two, three.
Footprints and abandoned castles and moats.
Seaweed turrets at day's end.

Sunday II

It was after the year had
nearly passed when the green grey oceanic day
laid its glassy magic down.
Waves washed the hours with cleansing balms
and the air drew mythical shapes from the headlands –
dragon ghosts, dogs and angels.
Figures in the distance
like small black shadows
stalking on their stilted legs,
the rustling of grassy dunes.

Return to the Sea

I waited for the sea
for the long months of winter
and dreamed of its salt and light
and the far far miles of sand
and its lull and hush,
I dreamed of it, and all
the muscles and sinews in my womb,
my hips and spine ached for the space
of the long far beach and the
lines and lines of waves awash with falling sun
and the lone gull
and the sky as wide and linear as the bay
and distant headlands bathed in gold
and the rhythmic ritual of the tide,
again and again crashing on the shore.
I dreamed, contracted and entrenched
of unfurling my legs on the long lone walk
and the place to breath and the solitude.
I waited.
I longed.
And then
I came out of the clouds, the mist and rain
through the forest as green as glass
and the mountains riven with storm,
and the sea I had waited for
was here.

As mighty and replete
with solitude and light as I imagined
and I learned that
my longing was real, and the need
was real and the air was mellow
and a small rainbow appeared above the cliffs,
just for a moment but enough
and there was nothing to do but
behold it
and let it seep into me like a salve or balm
and the tightness in my chest
undid itself into the giant sky
and I knew that what I dreamed
was real
and I was safely
amongst the sea and the lonely sky again
and free.

For Angela Merkel, on the death of Karlov

When your country
ignores the pleas of children and your master, a tyrant and despot
amongst a tyranny of despots and thieves,
then you may cross the road for the last time in a beautifully
    cut suit and waistcoat
elegant on your colossal frame
and walk into a pristine, yet surreal modernist Art Gallery in
    Ankara,
the Cagdas Sanat Merkezi
and before a cultured crowd make a short speech
to open a discreet and tasteful exhibition depicting Turkish
    photographs
of what turns out to be the countryside of your birth,
and an impeccably dressed handsome young man
in a dark suit with a crisp white shirt and dark slim tie
will shoot you in the back on behalf of Syria
And you will fall on the white floor before cameras and art,
and your blood will run across the white tiles
as the young man shouts for the millions of children
that you – as a representative of your country –
have let be killed.
A beautiful scene shot in black and white,
with the voluptuous swipe of red, a video clip, your death its
    own piece of art.
It looks like an installation – shall we call it
Death of Karlov at the hands of the Turks or
Death of Karlov in Ankara or
maybe just *Death of a Salesman*?
'Don't forget Aleppo,' shouts the beautiful young man before
    he himself is killed.

And on this same day,
a truck will ram into Christmas markets in
the forecourt of a Berlin cathedral,
and the horror that we long foresaw,
will spread like a virus
charting a course
that at last seems
unsurprising and then, inevitable.
And it seems it falls to Angela to take a stand, who must
    choose a very careful path
to our redemption – for she is best placed
in the dark valleys of the demons to find a reasoned middle
    ground,
born as she was in East Germany in the days before the
    Führer and
committed to Christian harmony in her stout, pragmatic and
    comforting way –
for as the Chancellor herself has said,
'we do not want to live paralysed by the fear of evil',
And this is true.

But I can't help but think that the actions of the young
    assassin – Melvut Mert Altintas –
a young policeman, noble and heroic boy – echo an earlier
    maverick –
Gavrilo Princip, though he was not a Turk but opposite and
    despised the Ottomans,
but still in their own way, they each made deeply considered
    individual choices
about how to change the world, and dared to act,

though the truth is never as clear, nor the answers as black
and white as
the beautiful violent death of Karlov.
See Omran Daqneesh, covered in the debris of a bomb that
killed his brother.
See Alan Kurdi sleeping on the beach.
No wonder Dear Chancellor, your body trembles, standing
with Macron and Putin at the Shrine.
(Since the death of Karlov, at least another 400,000 Syrians
have died;
Russian airstrikes have killed 20,000 alone, and most of these
are children.
But 16 million people died in World War I, and 75 million
in World War II.)

The Infinity Dialogues

You said Infinity means
everything that has happened and will happen
has to happen,
as a mathematical fact,
and physics says
that the same things, in any number of variations,
inevitably happen over and over again,
and because that can happen, it will.
So – anything that can happen
will happen because it has to,
and therefore – there is no meaning
and nothing matters.

And I said I can't agree with
your 'therefore', because it seems to me
that therefore much matters, because
it is inevitable and part of the great whole,
that it would matter,
and that I would say it does
because I have to, and you
refused convincing.

But still –
you spent hours and hours
tinkering and planning and digging and
pottering and testing and toiling –
to build a wind turbine – like
a tradesman, and a scientist, like an old man, and a boy –
completely absorbed and elemental
because it mattered, and you were happy because

the wind turbine caught the wind,
and because it was.

And you said –
everything is mathematics and calculus, the chances and
likelihoods, and there is nothing but science as a matter of
   lore and law.

And I said that is also just as plainly philosophy,
and the man who loves dogs and wind turbines – is a
philosopher as much as a simpleton, a tradesman and a
   physicist.

In defiance of meaning.

And I said – why are you drinking so much? And you said,
   I'm not, or
only as much as I need. And I let you. And I said – are you
   all right? And you lied,
and said 'yes', and I let you,
because it was the witching hour with the air like a crypt
   beyond the fire
and we had
been drinking all night, and talking
and because
I thought to lay down with you
to soothe the storms,
but could not, so
a late night lie
seemed the smallest concession to make
in the face of the great and sacred whole.

And you called me cunt – and that was as it should be,
because of infinity – and I let you
because…because it was complex,
and the anger was pure and
unadulterated,
the utter eloquence
and in that small word I knew the opposite
was also true, and its variations of feeling
and though you fought it, your anger
evinced the possibility of joy.

And it seemed
that ruminations on physics and infinity
were a way to assuage great dissolutions,
and to resile the pieces that won't fit, but must, and will
because they have to because of physics, because they can
therefore they will and have before, defiantly.
And it seemed also that the philosopher is one who,
when he looks at the stars,
feels both small, and comforted –

because all of that is out there and still, we exist –
because love and joy are inevitable and infinite and will
    always be expressed
mathematically or otherwise
in algorithms of breath and bone.

And the bush barely murmurs and
the fire makes a small crackle and warms the house,
and the croaking dam,
and the soughing wind…says

there is no need
to succumb
to nihilism and sadness when
there is so much yet to come
and I say so, ready
to bear witness when you fall apart,
because it will happen, because it has to,
though you try so hard to make it not matter
which is also inevitable.

And you seem wilfully to forget
that it's so simple, as simple
as a dog lying in the sun, or starlight on the gumtrees
before dawn –
the broken parapet beyond the ridge.
And in all the endless variations, and repetitions,
there is one constant and that is you, yourself,
as you are, the only one, once, and I, and each,
and in that minute particular the infinite universe
conspires.

*

And in your dream – you found a silver ring in the waters of
    the river
with a price tag tied to it that said '$204' (very specific).
But then the waters rose to a flood, rushing down the valley –
a deluge of brown water, and swept the ring away.
And, resolute, you set to walking through water and sludge,
looking for the ring, resolutely or resigned – I couldn't say –
and you wondered why.

But it seems clear
that the price tag is a symbol only
of that ascribed idea of value and meaning – and the ring
a silver circle – plain and clean – denoting infinity.
And it was washed from your grasp even as you tried to
    fathom it
And it was necessary that you searched, because
it meant something
and you searched down the river to find it
because it mattered – a search for meaning amid
waters of emotion that drown you in the dark.
But you need not be afraid, because you pressed on regardless
and were dogged, feeling driven – but not urgent…
though I don't know that for sure, for I don't know the
    feeling that it left
on your body on waking – if it was strength or fear
that gripped you in the pre-dawn light, but then,
comforted by the warm weight of dogs
and their guileless, unselfconscious breath.

And I don't know if you are reachable,
through the infinite realms of sadness,
though it is inevitable and will occur because it can,
and the mountains standing sentinel
and the infinite sky, curving
its way to the sea,
bear witness to what will be, circular and clear
like a bellbird, or a tear.

The Infinity Dialogues II

…and then you said

given infinity,
anything that can happen must happen
an endless number of times.

(in truth, an acknowledgement of mystery)

And you asked – If
an infinite number of universes drop out of
an infinite sea of energy (big bangs)
and then evaporate into nothing
then how can there be meaning?

(which I see is impossible for you to navigate
because so huge and hopeless in its premise
but also that your reasoning
is problematic,
because so infinite in its parameters,
and beyond a certain comprehension –
which is not the same as being beyond meaning –
and that which we do not understand is not
meaningless, but sometimes simply
more meaningful
than we can grasp)

And I also see
that the word 'If'
is in fact the secret caveat to your argument
because 'If' means we don't know the answer
and your language is spare and beautiful

as you express your longing for meaning
even within despair,
where even the word 'infinite' itself
is evocative and beautiful in its inscrutable
completeness.

And you say
that we materialise from energy,
concentrating it into a body/life, and return to
just that,
and that too is like a small poem, but also
somehow too utilitarian,
almost wilfully denying
the flesh and love that bring us into being
and reside in us, and too
the blood and bone and mind and passion of that life,
the singular humanity, the dreams

And you say there can be
no memory of the existence of life, a planet, a star system, a
   galaxy or a universe – for they're all temporary
over and over again.
But yet – but yet…
our stories plot memories that go back into the
Dreamtime and beyond, and in our muscle memory and in our
shared consciousness is the memory of great love,
and you say that meaning needs life to exist and seeing life's
   temporary then so is meaning but I say
if life equals meaning then meaning is everywhere
because life is all we have
and is its own meaning

and matters
as you matter
and as do I.

And there's a broken longing in your reasoning –
problematic because so infinite in its parameters
that it cannot face
the deeply intimate and particular –
and in that way you use
physics – that is built on a myriad of intimate particulars –
to render all the detail of this beauty obsolete…
but it is that beauty and belief that makes us real –
though much more frightening than nihilism,
which sometimes seems as though it is a way
to be free of truth – to say it doesn't matter
when it does.

And it seems it must be
the loneliness and the darkness of the bush at night
that makes a man think of the complete extinction of life,
or of the universe evaporating to the point where atoms can't
    exist and subatomic particles are light years apart
so that it
may as well be as if it never was…

and only God could fill that void
or love – and it seems that
meaninglessness is close to Godlessness
but maybe it is just sadness
that ripples through that long dark night
and takes away your will to try.

And – to think of all humanity, in its beautiful and intimate
    particularity,
moving to another Universe
in a sea of infinite universes in the search for meaning
is crazy, as you know it is,
and in fact the
perfect truth of infinity is this:
that we conjured Infinity from our own world and minds
and it is the concept of Everythingness and we grasp it within
    ourselves
and live it and express it in our own time and world
and in our bodies and our
imaginations
and it is simpler and more beautiful than even you
with your philosopher's heart can perceive.

And when your book is written
it should be hand-bound in leather
and written with a quill on parchment and it will be the book
of all the days and it will be mathematical and godly
and will become self-evident in its physics and its algebra.
Called 'Why the meaning of life = 0'.
Full of science and numbers like a magic sanscrit –
but you may find in the writing that it will transmogrify
into one word:
Infinity –
like the old man who wrote eternity on all the city streets
a simple, articulate and profound grace – and I will help you,
And in the writing you may find tears fall from your eyes
in recognition of the joy
of energy and matter

that you matter
and the meaning is within you
and in Pi and in the world
and in the heart and mountains

and is more easily discernible than
the endless unknown universes
of your imagination

and is warm
and safe
and simple

and the fear will then subside
and you will rest,
and see you cannot delay.

When Shall We Go?

(for John Clarke and Bryan Dawe)

When shall we go, John Clarke?
Not yet, surely?
But now – I see you knew that every moment was
but a preparation for this time, every word, every touch,
a preamble to the main.
To think – you stepped off on Palm Sunday, like the Lord,
walking in the Grampians, with your majestic aplomb
then came, poetically to Mount Abrupt, and then – were done.
Like a Holy One, preparing for death – our merriment, a true
blessing, anointed by our joy, and love.
Such love –
And so you knew every moment –
a precision instrument that bore the hallmarks of truth.
Now I see
predestination lit your casual glance, your quiet glee –
What fun, oh dearest man, what need, what true deceit
to think that it would ever be but this way – the steps toward
    ourselves
and separation made each moment holy thus.
I cannot bear the loss.
I just cannot,
but darling,
I see that you lived wholly in preparation for this time.
Deadpan and sweet – what joy.
And also – I want to discuss when next we meet:
Leaving on Palm Sunday! What?
No warning, and natural causes in your most beloved natural
    world!

So deeply felt.
And within the week Good Friday and God fall and his
 ascension, and you'll
be sleeping in the sod of green New Zealand then
as angels make to rise.
Surprise, oh but one more reprise?
When shall we go, dear John?
Not when you are ready, nor not I,
but when the gods decree, the sky.
But oh, not yet John Clarke, not yet – oh
so harshly rent, oh so abrupt.
My heart is broken though your love, it fills my cup
And overflows, and flow and flow –
You did not warn me you would go,
but still, come on, man, we should know –
One has to go on with the show.
The joy of you, oh joy, but first, this grief,
as raw and breathless as a body blow.

New Moon

Sliced into the velvet sky
a carving, a tattoo of light
a swathe of cloud like a great curtain
hung chiffon scarves giantly brushing
the mountains' black silhouette
etched sanscrit of trees
a tempest wind blowing
and the water so black
and cut with ribbons of neon light
sliced and carved with neon light
mysterious fear
a tattoo of the rippling low
in my heart.

The Valley

Stars and granite mark the path
to the mountain
and the pilgrimage
to the cold place
the path of the Valley People
Tidbinbilla, Ngunnawal, Tuggeranong, Namadgi, Birrigai.

Summer evening by the lake
after brutal heat, the evening.
A fish jumps from the water into evening air,
by the lake – leaving a ripple as it submerges itself again.
And in the shade of she-oaks the air takes on the water scent
as evening breezes rise in a coastal southerly way
and she-oak soughing begins, sister-singing and soft.

And the lake returns to its origins and
smells like the river recalling
long evenings long ago near brown water
and the symphony of bush birds – mopoke,
reign of the cockatoos, skirmishing gangs of
gang-gang and galah – making
wild evensong at eventide,
trilling to the sun that falls in gold as the wind rises,
and the reeds and rushes bow in the rush of evening air.

And the lake surface breaks and again with a brown-glass rippling
and the soughing rises to a keening and
giant evening dragonflies pit themselves against gusts
and it feels like a storm is storming in from the mountains
that cradle the lake and the valley in the ancient crook,

and I am within it on the lake's edge
catching solitude on the edge of the day
full of restless warning
as spring recklessly submits to an early summer
without fight, and Christmas a heartbeat away.

I try to listen to the tempest rising and absent myself,
merged into the ghostly breathing of the she-oaks and
the urgent bells of the silver birches' rush,
to not think of things that preoccupy me in their delay
and to let them falter and settle into the lake and into nothing
and will not matter in the end.

At peace, at peace – though the lake
is now so ruffled and restless and rising
and the mountains turn to darkness
and the pink light riffs against the cliffs far off
and down the sleepy valley to the far off sea,
somewhere far far away
far far away and gone
as past and future.

The summers they dare not speak of, bereft of hope

With the days as long as an age
stark, hot, hazy – a vision of a saga from ancient times
that we
Live
Through
where every step is a burden
of grey apocalyptic light heavy as dragged stone
to step and drag and step through-
a pilgrimage of broken thoughts
heat heat heavy as a sack
and winds raising the bad spirits
worrying the dust, the trees
worrying unseasonal pollens
driving
drying
The heart
Beating arrhythmic
Summer daze.

*

The Black Summer
koalas fell from the trees
firefighters dead in the battle
a million hectares razed to the ground.
It is Pompeii.
And the endless memory of smoke like an apocalypse,
　choking from the northern borders
all the way to the southern sea.

The Rural Fundamentalists II

We are the Rural Fundamentalists – hear our creed.
by day, the simple rhythms –
the stove to be lit by the wood to be chopped
from the logs to be gathered from beneath the trees
that have been grown and tended and then left to fall and dry
the grey of stone and sky and rusty iron red
to be gathered and chopped, to be gathered and stacked,
to roar in the woodstove, a hundred years the same,
a thousand.
Water to be drawn in the
big cast-iron kettle blackened by heat, to boil,
to make tea, to curl with steam, to comfort, and
the smell of smoke, the crackling of kindling
the cracking of eggs and the gathering of kin,
and the porcelain mixing bowls full of flour from the barrel,
baking and sweeping and cutting and folding
and hanging and smoothing and gathering and scattering.
The chooks to be called, and the scattering of grain scooped
from the big oil drum, drawing the tin cup through the rivers
   of gold,
the hushing of millions of pieces of wheat, soft and porous as
   sand, as soil,
'heeere chook, chook, chook' and the pecking of grain with their
darting intent hen-precision, brooding their satisfied noise
'brrrrrrrk, brrrrrrrk', soft and low, peck, and peck.
And hands at the apron and lowing of cows,
and perched on the stool, greasing the hands to pull at the teats
and the squirt of the milk brisk and hard
Ringing in the metal buckets, 'zzzzzt, zzzzzzt',

The scalding tea, and the sun like a jangling jubilant spirit
splitting the cool green horizon, spilling out from the hills
over the paddocks of gold, the rising of steam from the moist
   brown paddocks
the rich red soil, fertile and cobbled,
And the gentle flow of a mild winter over the nestled land.
The work, and the shovel and calloused hands,
and splinters and grease and oil and the strain and chink of
   the plough
and the rise of the morning into a gently burnished day.
These quiet times.
The quiet time.
The quietude that only the land and the bush can hold.
The strong back and the strong arms –
The times that fold over and over like a wave,
Quiet on quiet, the blue, blue sky, and the grey sky
And the far horizon – always the sky and
the far horizon – making you see the distance, making you small
making you safe and small –
And down and through like a wing
to the evenings of clatter and bustle, the fire cracking, the
   rocking chair
And the lamplight, and the darkling land taken by stealth, by the
Great Magisterial Night, and the warm bed
and the black, black velvet sky and the Universe and the
   million stars
And the cry of the lone owl, and the cry, the cry of the tawny
   frogmouth
sitting in trees and watching his kingdom
And the tangled dreams,

and sometimes, lightning to the north,
and blessed rain that moves over the land
like a great entourage, like a gathering of spirits,
leaving shadows…
Leaving trees uprooted, leaving a sweet hush below,
And the rhythms and turns of the harvest and the season,
And by night, whispered prayers, the secrets,
And the deep, sweet sleep in clean starched heavy sheets,
And the rising to greet each day as a blessing,
And the code of honour,
And the work of stewardship,
Stoicism and replenishment,
This – the foundation of everything we are.

The Rural Fundamentalists III

I grew up vast in silence, and attuned to the sound of that Land.
Notice: the shift of wind, the white noise of storms in gumtrees,
still water, riffling water, the ache of the sheep's maw in the dark,
the still air and the train coming for an age down the track before
it thunders through in the dark, through in a roar.
Imperceptible the imprint of light on my mind – the haze of
    coming rain,
the quenching lemon light of May, the darkling cloud from
    the north,
smell of dusty ichor on the air, sense of green in the
    cumulous, how brolgas once flew
through at Easter like the gods, the white light, the green, the
    purple and the deep grey,
and the shimmering satin light of late evening, and the blue
    midnight,
and the gold gold gold of Autumn, the gold sheen of cool dawn,
All. Nothing smells like the smell of the rain out here.

Summer is queen peaches like bulbs of sugar and sun,
    nectarines, blood plums,
apricots that taste of sex and dust, rich gold and dusty
    orchards full of Italian boys.
As a child I would wait all winter for that first smell, the early
    crop, the juice, the bite.
Harvest and laying and shearing, days into months, the ripe
    and the rugged, and jangly
Scrabbly, tumbling, rumbling, rambling. Summer is brown
    water, brown snakes, brown skin,
Lying glistening on the warm cement beside the pool,
    breathing your own breath against

The crook of your slim brown arm, the smell of wet warm
    chloriney cement, blue blue pool
Blue blue sky, blue, blue blinded.

The day starts with the lowing of cattle,
The rooster's crow and murmur of insects and sentinel birds,
and ends with the nesting of cockatoos high in the broken gums,
squawking and scratching and settling in.
Grain and flour and milling and ploughing and baking and
    herding
and pruning and crutching and offerings
to the gods in storage and cellars, the meats and the grains
in the sheds and the coolrooms,
Gathering tomatoes and making of sauces, rows of beautiful
jars of preserved fruit and tomatoes in the deep pantry,
And killing the fatted pig for the June salami ritual
And churning the butter and picking the fruit from the
    vineyards and orchards
And calling
Calling
Calling across paddocks, calling
and returning
Calling and returning again.
And again
And all that is true is in the soil
And the light and the heart
The patience, the fatalism, the battle and relinquishment.
Fundamental.
Immutable.

The Rural Fundamentalists IV

We are the Rural Fundamentalists – hear our creed.

I prefer outside walking
catching the rain on my face
and the sun on my skin
and the wind in my hair,
messy, wrecked and unadorned.

I prefer things that you do with your hands –
tangible, dirty and real,
splinters under my skin, dirt in my nails
digging, tying knots and cutting things, branches and wire
boots and a T-shirt, with my dog and the wide open spaces,
plain-faced.

I prefer plain food –
vegetables from the garden, strong cheese and heavy bread,
garlic, eggs and butter, beer, whiskey, meat from the
    paddock.
I prefer –
the pub to bars – that sacred ritual
coming in under the old veranda to the musty gloom
the fireplace and the pool table,
the smell of men and flannelette.

I prefer
Wood fire to gas.

I prefer candlelight and lamps.
I prefer the old velvet couch and tumbling pillows to clean lines.
I prefer handmade, hand-knitted, hand-spun
I prefer dirt and laughter and fumbling,
stubble, breath and morning kisses,
the smell of love on the warm sheets.
I prefer eggs warm, salvaged from hay in rusty drums,
brown and speckled and inside
as bright as a navel orange in winter sun.
I prefer bluntness, no pretence

I prefer
bare feet, wood smoke, the anvil and the axe
I choose space and light
I need movement, peace and grace.

I prefer
grey skies, clouds darkling, storm and tempest
and then the cool
morning, and the dew and light rising.

I prefer Nature's quiet, the silent paddocks
The breath and warmth of animals
and each day like a beautiful simple prayer.

The Manifesto of a Just Country

Protect all natural and cultural heritage as the highest priority, communicate that priority to the community:
- Great Barrier Reef and the Tarkine and the Burrup Peninsula
- all endangered species, including koalas, platypus, frogs, bilbies, parrots, fish, everything
- forests, rivers and the sea
- teach all children about the rare importance of the natural environment we must protect
- reinvest in environmental protection, remove the regulations that water down the definitions of 'heritage', and 'endangered'.

Create a Sustainable Agriculture Policy:
- recognise and enshrine all small hold farmers officially as Custodians of the Land and of food growing knowledge, place them at the highest end of knowledge
- link them with Elders and Indigenous bodies to work together as custodians of knowledge and practice
- pursue natural sequence farming (Peter Andrews), carbon farming and localised Landcare practice and water management.

Recognise the professions of care and knowledge and pay them what they are worth:
- protect teachers, nurses, paramedics, firefighters, police, doctors – the public service that they provide, the knowledge they carry, the heroism and protection they give us.

Protect and fund the ABC and uphold the diversity of the media, journalists and journalism:

- support public radio and small regional and independent newspapers, bolster Radio National and Radio Australia.

Spend large amounts of money on social housing projects (such as in Europe).

Link people who need jobs and housing with small country towns where there are lots of houses empty – set up cooperatives.

Enshrine protection of Libraries, Books, the Arts, Artists and music.

Protect our healthcare sector from privatisation.

Rightfully recognise and restore Indigenous Sovereignty:
- create Indigenous Elders Consultative Council – to oversee policy and legislation for all policy across all governments – advice and guidance like with Circular Justice, to protect land and habitat, to be just and non-corrupt
- teach Indigenous language, culture, history in all school K-6, and high schools
- recognise and identify languages and language groups in all schools
- invite Elders to teach and lead at all schools.

Teach music to every student.

Remove all children from detention.

Rebuild our manufacturing sector and protect Australia from foreign buyouts, including our farmland, our water and our other natural assets and infrastructure.

Breaking the Golden Rule: love in the time of Covid-19

My true love is on the front line of this war –
I'm so scared, I pray for him.
He says we can't fuck because of coronavirus
while he stands two feet away undressing me with his
 beautiful eyes,
untouchable.
It makes me want to kill myself.
I think, 'I so need him in me now when the
world is all strange and out of kilter, spiralling.'
The only thing that matters at the end of the world is being
 close together,
but now, that seems the hardest to grant.
I tell him, 'I'd rather die of the virus than not be allowed
to fuck you', even though I know it's crazy, but not, I want
 him need him
and would die for him anyway, waiting, waiting. I think in circles.
For the world to go to shit and not be able to hold him,
and then to die anyway without the final months of joy – is
unthinkable, the final months
when we would do anything, where there would be nothing
 to lose, and
we would shed the last veils of secrecy and be utterly naked
 together,
and do everything
and nothing would break us, heart-bound – camped in the
 elements,
hunting for food, and making love at the end of the world
– the only thing that would carry us out of the shadows
into the light of redemption.

www.ingramcontent.com/pod-product-compliance
Lightning Source LLC
Chambersburg PA
CBHW070938080526
44589CB00013B/1555